# MY VOICE

Edited By Iain McQueen

First published in Great Britain in 2022 by:

Young Writers
Remus House
Coltsfoot Drive
Peterborough
PE2 9BF
Telephone: 01733 890066
Website: www.youngwriters.co.uk

Printed and bound in the UK by BookPrintingUK
Website: www.bookprintinguk.com
YB0492K

# FOREWORD

For Young Writers' latest competition This Is Me,
we asked primary school pupils to look inside
themselves, to think about what makes them unique,
and then write a poem about it! They rose to the
challenge magnificently and the result is this fantastic
collection of poems in a variety of poetic styles.

Here at Young Writers our aim is to encourage creativity
in children and to inspire a love of the written word, so
it's great to get such an amazing response, with some
absolutely fantastic poems. It's important for children to
focus on and celebrate themselves and this competition
allowed them to write freely and honestly, celebrating
what makes them great, expressing their hopes and
fears, or simply writing about their favourite things.
This Is Me gave them the power of words. The result
is a collection of inspirational and moving poems that
also showcase their creativity and writing ability.

I'd like to congratulate all the young poets
in this anthology, I hope this inspires them
to continue with their creative writing.

# CONTENTS

| | |
|---|---|
| Annie Rice | 77 |
| Kali Napier (10) | 78 |
| Megan Linch (8) | 79 |
| Melina Tuyluoglu (8) | 80 |
| Dexter Newby-Walker (8) | 81 |
| Connie Shepherd (9) | 82 |
| Rocco Pillay (7) | 83 |
| Sienna Amin (7) | 84 |
| Eva Grutzner (7) | 85 |
| Samuel Webb (9) | 86 |
| Lilah Piper (8) | 87 |
| Evie Makinson (10) | 88 |
| Henry Saunt (9) | 89 |
| Emily Benzeval (7) | 90 |
| Daniella Foxcroft (10) | 91 |
| Ava Dockery (7) | 92 |
| Josh Lines (8) | 93 |
| Jessica Beattie (7) | 94 |
| Harrison Plant (8) | 95 |
| Sienna Culm (7) | 96 |
| Lola Howes (10) | 97 |
| Niall Smit (9) | 98 |
| Frank Linch (7) | 99 |

## Barcroft Primary School, Barcroft

| | |
|---|---|
| Marlie Bailey (8) | 100 |
| Mansa Kaur Chahal (8) | 101 |
| Colby-Blu Read (8) | 102 |
| Amandeep Kaur (8) | 103 |
| Akaal Singh Dhillon (8) | 104 |
| Ethan Gregory (8) | 105 |
| Jovan Ashan (8) | 106 |
| Lotti Harrison (9) | 107 |
| Riley Morris (8) | 108 |
| Carla-Maria Berechet (8) | 109 |
| Bradley Thomas Dunn (8) | 110 |
| Ekam Singh Badyal (8) | 111 |
| Sophia Zaman (8) | 112 |
| Riley Makin (8) | 113 |
| Perran Peters (8) | 114 |
| Jasroop Singh (9) | 115 |
| Logan Seaton (8) | 116 |

## Snainton CE Primary School, Snainton

| | |
|---|---|
| Jack Watson (9) | 117 |
| Hannah Boynton (8) | 118 |
| Katy Goodrick (8) | 119 |
| Connie Harber (7) | 120 |
| Oskar Bond (8) | 121 |
| Jessica Hodgson (10) | 122 |
| Clifford Akrill (7) | 123 |
| Charleigh Jones (10) | 124 |
| Imogen Parkin (8) | 125 |
| Scarlett Freer (9) | 126 |
| Kasper Reeve (7) | 127 |
| Christopher Boynton (9) | 128 |
| Madelaine Jenkins (8) | 129 |
| Jessica Berry (10) | 130 |
| Oliver Osborne (10) | 131 |
| Isaiah Jones (7) | 132 |

## Walgrave Primary School, Walgrave

| | |
|---|---|
| Mollie-Mae Brown (10) | 133 |
| Ewan McGillivary (11) | 134 |
| Martha Burchell (10) | 136 |
| Imogen Perkins (11) | 138 |
| Lucie Cawston (9) | 140 |
| Thomas Sweeney (10) | 142 |
| Ella Sargent (10) | 144 |
| Mark Spatcher (9) | 146 |
| Irene Alvarez (9) | 147 |
| Jenson Budd (9) | 148 |
| Faith Wharton (10) | 149 |
| Mackenzie Thomas Wainwright (10) | 150 |
| Elly-Mae Potts (10) | 151 |
| Isla Mulligan (10) | 152 |
| Devlyn Morrison (10) | 153 |

## Ysgol Calon Y Dderwen, Newtown

| | |
|---|---|
| Laci Phillips (10) | 154 |
| Bradley Mitchell (10) | 156 |

| | |
|---|---|
| Leo Andrews (11) | 158 |
| Siena Salvati (11) | 159 |
| Leal Borysiewicz (10) | 160 |
| Jayden Ridgeway (10) | 162 |
| Aidan Owen (10) | 163 |
| Alex Riordan (10) | 164 |
| Jamie-Lee Ainsworth (11) | 165 |
| Kacey Jayne Dorrell (10) | 166 |
| Maddie Meller (10) | 167 |
| Charlie Cleaver (10) | 168 |
| Alfie Cleaver (10) | 169 |
| Emily Jerman (10) | 170 |

## Ysgol Gwaun Cae Gurwen, Gwaun Cae Gurwen

| | |
|---|---|
| Jac Davies Lewis (10) | 171 |
| Evie Williams | 172 |
| Jordan Challis (10) | 173 |
| Steffan Thomas (10) | 174 |
| Loti O'Sullivan (10) | 175 |
| Chris Preston (10) | 176 |
| James Gravil (10) | 177 |
| Alys Eira Lewis-Jones (8) | 178 |
| Wil Davies-Lewis (8) | 179 |
| Corey Evans (9) | 180 |
| Gethin Ieuan Hollis James (10) | 181 |
| Maddison Roberts (9) | 182 |
| Ellie Walker (9) | 183 |
| Harley Davies (10) | 184 |
| Alex White (10) | 185 |
| Dilan Morgan | 186 |
| Poppy Flood | 187 |
| Lucas Johns (9) | 188 |
| Ruby Osborne | 189 |

# THE POEMS

# The Journey Of Life

I breathe my first breath and smile,
People beaming down like waves towering over,
With legs that feel like jelly,
I step onto the station,
My life has started.

The train scampers on into my life,
Birthdays and sports days sprint through my head
in the form of a rainbow,
The train halts and pulls into the station,
Reading, drama, friends, wobbling along the
balancing beam.

Ahead of me, my life awaits,
I rush down a track to a part-time job,
Tensely running towards a portal of achievement,
Will I succeed?

As the train continues, the tracks get bumpier and
rockier,
Creating my career and banishing my old one,
Writing, illustrating, loving, I've drawn my future,
I take a breath and smile at my new life.

**Emily Frances Clay (10)**
Althorpe & Keadby Primary School, Keadby

# The Train Of Life

I take my first look and cry out,
I see black and white faces,
I've never seen it before,
In my favourite pair of shoes, I take my first wobbly
step onto the train platform,
My adventure is ahead of me,

The train gallops off towards the next adventure,
Halloween, Christmas and birthday parties race
past my view,
Spark of colours fly by,
As the train starts to stop and,
Pulls up into the station,
I sit up,
Is this me?
Speech and drama, horse riding and achievements,
Long peaceful days on bike rides.

In front of me, my next adventure awaits,
Racing down the track across fields of
achievements,

Nervously charging into battle with my stationary,
Ready next to me,
Will I succeed?

The train continues like thunder and lightning,
Busy carving my family and designing my career,
Horse riding, hiking, learning,
I take a look and smile.

**Neveah Whattam (10)**
Althorpe & Keadby Primary School, Keadby

# The Train Of Life

I feel myself lift up. As I open my eyes, I cry,
Black and white images beam down like sunshine,
In my brand-new trainers, I take my first step,
Then I stepped on the train,
The train creaked forward.

The train flew by like a reindeer,
Waiting for the next adventure,
Birthdays, Christmas and Halloween,
Celebrations and bike rides on the roads,
Netball, football and PE with my headteacher,
Long, sunny days with yummy ice pops.

Ahead of me, my adventure awaits,
Running down the track past acres of hormones,
Nervously passing where I want to be,
I want to succeed,
Will I get to where I want to be?

The train continues faster,
Than the speed of a lightning ball,

Designing my family and creating my business,
Cooking, cleaning and working,
I take a breath and smile.

**Katelyn Louise Padbury (10)**
Althorpe & Keadby Primary School, Keadby

# The Train Of Life

I look around and see a sea of faces and smile
away
Black and white scents and a beam of light
That starts my life

On my newborn legs, I crawl onto the platform and
step on the train,
I feel the train speeding off,
My life is waiting for me.

Siblings, celebrations, a rainbow of memories fly
by,
The train has slowed down and pulls into a new
step in life,
Friends, English, maths, long sunny lunches with
friends,

Ahead of me, my adulthood awaits,
Sprints down on the track past puddles of
memories,
Nervously running to battle with books and
stationery in hand,
Will I succeed?

The train continues at the speed of light,
Designing my YouTube career and family,
My driving license and YouTube account,
I take a breath and smile.

**Dylan White (10)**
Althorpe & Keadby Primary School, Keadby

# Platform Four

As I take a breath and look around,
Eyes beam like rays of sunlight in black and white
images.

In new shoes, a step is taken,
The whistle is blown,

The train sprints towards the unknown,
The stabilisers come off my bike,
Celebrations and family trips are memories that
will,
Be remembered for an eternity of love,

The train reaches its next adventure,
As the cake spells out happy birthday,
The drama begins,

Trodding past acres of mood swings,
Nervously running forwards,
Awaiting the portal of achievements,
Will I succeed?

The train continues faster than a lightning bolt,
Mapping my career and designing my family,
Engineering, laughing, loving,
I take a breath and smile.

## Libby Fowles (11)

Althorpe & Keadby Primary School, Keadby

# Life Of Me

I take a small breath and my eyes open,
My first ever words sing out of me like a musical
play,
Then my feet moved like jelly and I move into the
spotlight,
My journey awaits.

The train gallops through my life,
I end up at this unknown building called school,
Sunny days playing with friends on the field and in
the willow,
Friends, family and big adventures,
Long seasons with flowers, conkers and snowy
trees,

Secondary school is ahead of me, just waiting,
Will I make friends?
My exams are waiting for me as I go into battle
with my pen,
Will I pass?

This journey gets challenging as it continues
moulding my life and creating, my world,
Singing, dancing, loving,
I take a deep breath and smile.

## Krystal Proctor (10)
Althorpe & Keadby Primary School, Keadby

# Train Journey

I take my first breath and cry out,
I am alone, surrounded by the sunshine of faces I barely know,
On spaghetti-like legs, I take my first steps onto the platform,
The whistle is blown.

The train gallops off the moment I step on,
Holidays and family time, a row of pictures fly by,
The train slows down to the next chapter,
Beaches, sleepovers, pets, long sunny days at school.

Ahead of me, my next chapter awaits,
Sprinting down the track past tons of hormones,
Nervously, running towards a portal of sudden respectfulness,
Will I get to where I want to be?

The train continues to the next chapter,
Designing my life and creating a family,
Vet, loving, learning,
I close my eyes and smile.

## Roxanna May Quinn (10)

Althorpe & Keadby Primary School, Keadby

# Train Of Life

I wake to see a bright light that blinds me,
A shadowy figure imagines me as their god,
In my new shoes, I take my first steps onto the platform,
Life is now on.

The train sprints into action,
Moments later, Christmases and holidays dash by,
The train brakes, throwing me forward,
Who am I?
Friends, shows, achievements, how did I get here?
The train sprints into action seconds later.

Ahead of me, my future awaits me,
The train sprints past acres of despair,
Nervously battling tests with pen in hand,
When will it end?

The train stops at the end of the track,
I am now an adult,
Building, welding and coding,
I take a breath and wonder what I have become.

## Matthew Tong (10)
Althorpe & Keadby Primary School, Keadby

# The Train Of Life

I take my first breath and cry out,
Black and white images beam down at me like sunshine,
In my brand-new shoes, I take my first steps onto the platform, the whistle is blown,

The train dashes onto the next chapter,
Celebrations and family visits,
The train slows for the next station,
Teacher, friends, adventures,

Memories made at the park,
Ahead of me, my future as a teenager,

Sprinting down the track, past a bundle of hormones,
Anxiously running towards a portal of exams,
Will I make it?

The train continues faster than the speed of a bolt,
Creating my path and designing my life,
Loving, working, learning,
I take a calm breath and smile.

## Kelsey Melissa Davidson (10)
Althorpe & Keadby Primary School, Keadby

# The Train Of Life

I take my first breath and open my eyes,
Nothing but black and white figures moving
towards me,
With my new shoes on I take my steps on the
platform,
This is just the beginning,
The train gallops on acceleration towards memory
lane,
Celebrating and family trips, every good memory,
the train slows to the next station,
Family, friends, enjoying the sunny outdoors,
Beyond my childhood is a file of responsibilities,
Sprinting down the track is a river of hormones,
Nervously, running through a dimension of
achievements
Will I succeed?
The train is going so fast, it's faster than light,
designing my career and modelling my life,
Reflecting on the world I created and I smile.

## Alfie Rusling (10)
Althorpe & Keadby Primary School, Keadby

# The Train Of Life

As I take a breath, my eyes open,
A wave of faces who I don't know staring down at me,
On wobbling legs, I take my first steps to the platform,
My life has started!

The train dashes off towards the unknown,
Birthdays and Halloweens pass by,
The train slows to the next chapter,
Teachers, sports, friends, long rainy days on the playground,

Ahead of me, my future awaits,
I race down the track of emotions,
Frantically I run towards a portal of decisions,
Will I pass?

As the train continues, the tracks get bumpier and rockier,
Creating my career and my life,
Art, acting, learning,
I take a breath and smile.

**Lilly Sophia Webster (10)**
Althorpe & Keadby Primary School, Keadby

# The Train Of Life

I take my first breath and cry for the first time,
Black and white faces look at me,
In my brand-new shoes, I take my first step onto
the platform,
The whistle was blown.

As the train gallops towards the unknown, it starts
to slow for the next chapter,
Sports, friends, long beautiful days with family,
Ahead of me, my journey of being a teenager
begins, sprinting down the tracks.

I look out the window and see acres of emotions,
Nervously sprinting to a portal of where I want to
be,
Will I achieve?

The train continues, storming down the rails,
My career and building my family,
I take a breath and smile.

**Brody MacLean (11)**
Althorpe & Keadby Primary School, Keadby

# All About Me

*A kennings poem*

A bee lover,
A zoo lover,
A swimming lover,
A poodle lover,
A cocker spaniel lover,
A school lover,
A French beginner,
A scaredy cat,
A Halloween lover,
A Christmas spirit,
A noodle lady,
A good friend,
A friend lover,
A born worrier,
A supportive friend,
A football fan,
A cockapoo stroker,
A family carer,
A Minecraft builder,
A Roblox player,

A smarty pants,
A cockapoo lover,
A pancake eater,
A Dr Pepper sipper,
A milkshake monster,
A chicken hater,
A fast runner,
A fish hater,
A fishing hater,
A summer lover.

## Lacey Jollands (10)

Althorpe & Keadby Primary School, Keadby

# This Is Me

I may be in Year 3,
However, I am a champion at dancing for England,
Making my way through the doors for a golden trophy,
I may be in Year 3,
Although I am an expert at horse riding,
Jumping my way through the glossy, emerald-green field,
I may be in Year 3,
But I'm a brilliant runner,
I'm as fast as a spotted cheetah after its terrified prey,
I may be in Year 3,
But I am an excellent egg seller,
Making everyone smile with excitement,
I may be in Year 3,
However, I'm a fabulous quadbike rider,
Making myself filthy like a disgusting pig rolling around in the mud.

**Lilly Broadbent (7)**
Althorpe & Keadby Primary School, Keadby

# The Train Of Life

I take my first gasp and I cry out,
Unrecognisable faces stare at me like I am their god,
In my new shoes, I step onto the train,
My life is ahead of me,
Special memories fly past me, a colourful rainbow is formed by happiness and joy,
Then it slows down at the next destination,
Life is getting harder, will I achieve?

Ahead of me, my future awaits,
Nervously running to a portal of achievements,
Will I succeed?

The train moves faster than the speed of light,
Moulding my life and making my family,
engineering, learning, travelling,
The end is near.

## Lucas Wall (10)
Althorpe & Keadby Primary School, Keadby

# All About Ebony

*A kennings poem*

A football fan,
A Minecraft machine,
An anxious ant,
A page turner,
A milkshake sipper,
A dog lover,
A laughing monster,
A pizza eater,
A chicken hater,
A lollipop licker,
A born worrier,
A conversation seeker,
A family carer,
A friend hugger,
A secret keeper,
A nature nerd
A school learner
A French beginner
A skateboard noob

A swimming starter
A cat hater
A Christmas spirit
A noodle slurper.

## Ebony Easthope (9)
Althorpe & Keadby Primary School, Keadby

# All About Alyx

*A kennings poem*

An attention seeker,
A dodgeball lover,
A born worrier,
A friend carer,
A family hugger,
A laugh lover,
A Coke sipper,
A dog owner,
An animal lover,
A caring sibling,
A Jack Russell stroker,
A BFF lover,
A good helper,
An amazing person,
A confident worrier,
A courageous fighter,
A smile sharer,
A food liker,
A heroic person,

A joke maker,
A quick thinker,
A sofa hogger,
A dancing queen.

## Alyx Brothwell (9)

Althorpe & Keadby Primary School, Keadby

# All About Addison

*A kennings poem*

A cheerleading lover,
A Fortnite player,
A Coke sipper,
A laugh giver,
A Rottweiler stroker,
A hamster holder,
A running superstar,
A sibling caller,
A fun baker,
A football player,
A fish owner,
A Twix adorer,
A singing hater,
An energetic runner,
A born worrier,
An attention seeker,
A friend lover,
A kind carer,
A secret keeper,
A sofa hogger,

A joke maker,
A quick thinker.

## Addison Hance (9)
Althorpe & Keadby Primary School, Keadby

# This Is Me

I may be in Year 3,
But I am a scientist at Spider-Man, shooting
imaginary webs,
I may be in Year 3,
But I am a pro gamer,
I may be in Year 3,
But I am a master parkourist, flipping and jumping
around,
I may be in Year 3,
But I am an amazing boxer, stronger than John
Cena,
I may be in Year 3,
But I can build like a construction builder,
I may be in Year 3,
But I am a pro gamer, building things in Minecraft.

## Leo Couch (7)

Althorpe & Keadby Primary School, Keadby

# The Train Of Life

I open my eyes and take my first breath,
Bright lights like sunshine beam down on me.

I step onto the platform with my shaky legs,
My life is waiting for me.

The train sprints towards the unknown,
A colourful rainbow forms from the memories and happiness,
The train slows down for the next destination,
Friends, sport and independence,
Fun times playing with people on games from all over the world.

## Isabelle Whitlam (10)
Althorpe & Keadby Primary School, Keadby

# Excellent Me

I may be in Year 3,
However, I am a fabulous runner, like a cheetah
running in the wind,
I may be in Year 3,
But I am amazing at Rockstars, I play my way
through the levels,
I may be in Year 3,
However, I am a wonderful dancer, dancing my
way through the stage like a champion dancer,
I may be in Year 3,
However, I am an excellent baker, creating great
strawberry cakes like Mary Berry.

## Willow Nutt (7)

Althorpe & Keadby Primary School, Keadby

# This Is Me

I may be in Year 3,
But I am a champion builder,
Building my way through the weather,
I may be in Year 3,
However, I am an amazing jumper,
I can jump to Saturn,
I may be in Year 3,
Yet I am a fantastic brother, hugging my sister like
a squishy marshmallow,
I may be in Year 3,
Although I am an excellent learner,
I am smarter than Albert Einstein.

## Henry (7)
Althorpe & Keadby Primary School, Keadby

# This Is Me

I may be in Year 3,
But I am a master at football,
I play better than Harry Kane,
I may be in Year 3,
However I am an excellent runner,
Running against other schools,
I may be in Year 3,
But I am an amazing tennis player,
Against my dad,
I may be in Year 3,
Yet I am an excellent skipper,
Skipping around the playground like a jumping bear.

## Jacob Waddingham (7)
Althorpe & Keadby Primary School, Keadby

# All About Lincoln

*A kennings poem*

A hot chocolate lover,
A hamster owner,
A Minecraft lover,
A good hugger,
A Lego builder,
A galaxy groover,
A brother hater,
A math questioner,
A YouTuber lover,
A cat stroker,
A McDonald's lover,
A Christmas getter,
A good helper,
A sofa hogger,
A slow thinker,
A maths lover,
An amazing artist.

## Lincoln Alexander Chapman (9)
Althorpe & Keadby Primary School, Keadby

# All About Me

I may be in Year 3
But I am fantastic at counting in French, as fluent
as the Eiffel Tower
I may be in Year 3
However, I adore kittens, like an expert pet carer
I may be in Year 3
Yet I am brilliant at art, like Jackson Pollock
splattering paint all around the canvas
I may be in Year 3
Although I am a champion cartwheeler, like
Shannon Miller.

## Rosabella Hazon (8)

Althorpe & Keadby Primary School, Keadby

# This Is Me

I may be in Year 3,
But I am an excellent jumper, bouncing around like a rabbit,
I may be in Year 3,
But I am an excellent trick-or-treater, filling up my bucket with sweets,
I may be in Year 3,
But I am a master fossil hunter like Mary Anning,
I may be in Year 3,
But I am a champion bike rider, riding up to Keadby from West Butterwick.

## Lexi Dixon (7)
Althorpe & Keadby Primary School, Keadby

# This Is Me

I may be in Year 3,
However, I am an amazing nail artist,
I may be in Year 3,
But I am an expert bike rider,
I may be in Year 3,
However, I love swimming in pools,
I may be in Year 3,
But I love going in the hot tub,
I may be in Year 3,
Yet I love doing flips and tricks on my trampoline,
And cartwheels on the grass.

## Yasmine Couch (7)

Althorpe & Keadby Primary School, Keadby

# This Is Me

I may be in Year 3,
But I'm a master hopper, hopping all around the
world like a kangaroo.

I may be in Year 3,
However, I am the most imaginative person in the
world.

I may be in Year 3,
But I am the best runner, running around the
world.

I may be in Year 3,
But I am a master biker, biking around the world.

## Isaac Hopkins (7)
Althorpe & Keadby Primary School, Keadby

# All About Me

*A kennings poem*

A Roblox lover,
A family hugger,
A Coke sipper,
An animal lover,
A hamster holder,
A cat lover,
A noodle licker,
A good helper,
A cousin caller,
A sassy queen,
A good singer,
A dog trainer,
A born stresser,
A chocolate eater,
A phone lover,
A noisy pupil,
A sofa hogger.

## Alyssia Thompson (9)
Althorpe & Keadby Primary School, Keadby

# This Is Me

I may be in Year 3
Yet I am a brilliant artist, painting like Picasso
I may be in Year 3
But I am an excellent runner like a zooming car
I may be in Year 3
However, I am an amazing reader, like Fulica
Donald
I may be in Year 3
All the same, I am a fantastic hopper, hopping
around the playground like a kangaroo.

**Maisie McGugan (7)**
Althorpe & Keadby Primary School, Keadby

# Excellent Me

I may be in Year 3,
However, I am an excellent runner,
I'm as fast as a car,
I may be in Year 3,
I'm a champion reader,
I may be in Year 3,
But I am a champion artist,
Like Jackson Pollock splashing paint,
I may be in Year 3,
However, I am an excellent dancer,
Like a hip-hop person.

**Roscoe Murray (7)**
Althorpe & Keadby Primary School, Keadby

# All About Paige

*A kennings poem*

A cat napper,
A horse rider,
An intelligence giver,
A vegetable hater,
A knowledge nicker,
A collie keeper,
An amazing sister,
A passionate person,
A Lego lover,
A huge hugger,
A curry keeper,
A tail wagger,
A sofa hogger,
A quick thinker,
A game player.

## Paige White (9)
Althorpe & Keadby Primary School, Keadby

# All About Harry

*A kennings poem*

A Lego lover,
A burger lover,
A Minecraft player,
A Fortnite player,
An Among Us player,
A science guy,
A Roblox player,
A maths guy,
A hungry person,
A crazy man,
A Fanta drinker,
A McDonald's lover,
A Subway lover,
A school lover,
A chicken eater.

## Harry Hopkins (9)
Althorpe & Keadby Primary School, Keadby

# All About Me

*A kennings poem*

A cat lover,
A lasagne eater,
A Coke sipper,
A teddy hugger,
A born runner,
A friend carer,
A page turner,
An information writer,
A smile giver,
A space wanderer,
A family carer,
A swimming lover,
A warm lover,
A Halloween scarer,
A chihuahua wanter.

**Izabelle Treacy (9)**
Althorpe & Keadby Primary School, Keadby

# All About Me

*A kennings poem*

A dog stroker,
A lemonade lover,
A noodle eater,
A sister hugger,
A game player,
A rabbit lover,
A Minecraft builder,
A monopoly player,
A secret warrior,
A song writer,
A fast runner,
A game winner,
A chicken lover,
A person hugger,
A dancing queen.

## Faith Storr (9)
Althorpe & Keadby Primary School, Keadby

# All About Afonso

*A kennings poem*

A cat stroker,
An amazing friend,
A Fortnite player,
A Minecraft builder,
An Among Us player,
A good Robloxer,
An amazing helper,
A brave brain,
A cinema person,
A McDonald's lover,
A rocket lover,
A space lover,
A school student,
A page turner.

## Afonso Figueiredo (9)
Althorpe & Keadby Primary School, Keadby

# All About Harriet

*A kennings poem*

A joke maker,
A secret keeper,
A book worm,
A big sister,
An attention seeker,
A BFF lover,
A smile giver,
An information sharer,
A cake lover,
A Coke sipper,
A dog hugger,
A good writer,
A KFC lover,
A TikTok master,
A curry lover.

**Harriet Waddingham (10)**
Althorpe & Keadby Primary School, Keadby

# Excellent Me

I may be in Year 3,
Although I am an expert at fishing salmon in the rainforest, I catch them with my bare hands,
I may be in Year 3,
But I am an amazing player at Rockstar, rocking like a rock god,
I may be in Year 3,
However, I am a master at looking after my pet like a vet.

## Jack Geldart (7)
Althorpe & Keadby Primary School, Keadby

# This Is Me

I may be in Year 3,
But I am a master monster truck controller,
I may be in Year 3,
Yet I am amazing at flying, I can go so high,
I may be in Year 3,
However, I drive a race car for England,
I may be in Year 3,
Although I ride a hot air balloon to the moon.

## Jace Jollands (8)
Althorpe & Keadby Primary School, Keadby

# Things About Me

*A kennings poem*

A dog chaser
An animal lover
A Roblox player
A cake eater
A dog stroker
A small person
A Coke sipper
An owl lover
A maths leader
A hug giver
A helper
A vampire watcher
A red lover
A quick runner
A lone thinker.

**Ella Davey (9)**
Althorpe & Keadby Primary School, Keadby

# Piper

I may be in Year 3,
But I am a champion at front flips,
I can flip from home to my grandma's,
I may be in Year 3,
But I can jump to the moon and back,
I may be in Year 3,
However, I am the greatest at biking to the church
hall and back.

## Piper Britcliffepeal (7)
Althorpe & Keadby Primary School, Keadby

# All About Me

*A kennings poem*

A budgie owner,
A Fortnite player,
A Minecraft builder,
A Roblox diva,
A page turner,
A cucumber eater,
A horse lover,
A coffee sipper,
A knowledge soaker,
A care giver,
A multiplication master,
An only daughter.

## Mercy Broughton (10)
Althorpe & Keadby Primary School, Keadby

# This Is Me

This is me...
My eyes are as brown as a monkey,
My hair is as blonde as a hamster,
I'm a wolf, hear my howl, I'll hunt you down,
My skin is as white as a rabbit,
My smile is as big as a crocodile,
My laugh is as good as a hyena.

**Indiyana Blewett (8)**
Althorpe & Keadby Primary School, Keadby

# All About Me

I may be in Year 3,
However, I am a champion runner, running all over the field,
I may be in Year 3,
But I love animals, watching them around the wildlife,
I may be in Year 3,
However, I am the fastest swimmer, swimming like a shark.

## Lotty Hampshire (8)

Althorpe & Keadby Primary School, Keadby

# All About Me

*A kennings poem*

A caring sibling,
A bike lover,
A sleep lover,
A good friend,
A loud caller,
A Minecraft lover,
A Roblox player,
A cake maker,
A pet owner,
An animal lover,
A caring best friend.

## Tegan Tyrell (9)

Althorpe & Keadby Primary School, Keadby

# Everything About My Life

*A kennings poem*

A milkshake sipper,
A sister hugger,
A Barbie player,
A quiet speaker,
A good crafter,
An excellent baker,
A page turner,
A little sibling,
A game winner,
An animal stroker.

## Sophie Groarke (9)
Althorpe & Keadby Primary School, Keadby

# All About Me

*A kennings poem*

A pizza lover,

A dog hugger,

An Xbox player,

A bike rider and scooter rider,

A chip muncher,

A sofa hogger,

A blanket hugger,

A Minecraft player,

A picnic lover.

## Tyler Brocklesby (9)

Althorpe & Keadby Primary School, Keadby

# This Is Me

I may be in Year Three
But I am a champion athletic runner, getting a
gold medal
I may be in Year Three
But I am a master skateboarder, like Tony Hawks.

## Ashdon Manning (7)

Althorpe & Keadby Primary School, Keadby

# This Is Me

This is me...
My eyes are as green as emeralds
I am as strong as a lion, hear me roar
I'm as fast as a cheetah
I'm as tiny as a mouse.

## Cassie Dalton (8)

Althorpe & Keadby Primary School, Keadby

# This Is Me

This is me...
I am as tall as a tree
I am a wise old owl
My eyes are as blue as a blue snowflake
My ears are as big as the bright sun.

## Megan Askham (8)
Althorpe & Keadby Primary School, Keadby

# This Is Me

This is me...
I am as small as a snake,
I am a monkey,
My speed is as fast as a kangaroo's,
My strength is like a lion's.

**Elliot Alexander (8)**
Althorpe & Keadby Primary School, Keadby

# This Is Me

This is me...
I am as fast as a cheetah
I am as tall as a tree
My ears are as little as a mouse
My feet are as strong as steel.

## Harry Whitehouse (8)
Althorpe & Keadby Primary School, Keadby

# This Is Me

This is me...
I am as small as a mouse,
I am a star,
My eyes are as brown as a tree trunk,
My voice is as quiet as a whisper.

## Summer Barnaby (9)
Althorpe & Keadby Primary School, Keadby

# This Is Me

This is me...
I am as fast as a lightning strike
I am an explosion
My hair is as brown as the wood
My eyes are brown marbles.

## Charlie Brelsford (8)

Althorpe & Keadby Primary School, Keadby

# This Is Me

This is me...
I am as hot as a burning fire
I am a very pink flamingo
My hair is as brown as chocolate
My lips are red roses.

**Kimmy Bailey (8)**
Althorpe & Keadby Primary School, Keadby

# This Is Me

This is me...
I am as small as a whiteboard,
I am like lightning,
My eyes are as blue as the ocean,
My feet are cheetah feet.

## Lucas Morfitt (8)
Althorpe & Keadby Primary School, Keadby

# This Is Me

This is me...
I am as vivid as a peacock,
I am a funny monkey,
My hair is as dark as dark chocolate,
I'm a night star.

## Leonor Meias (7)
Althorpe & Keadby Primary School, Keadby

# This Is Me

This is me...
I am a footballer
My smile is as big as a football
My voice is a deep song
I am as smart as a bee.

**Fynley Isaac (9)**
Althorpe & Keadby Primary School, Keadby

# This Is Me

This is me...
I am as tall as a giraffe
I'm a gorilla
My speed is as fast as a fairy
My strength is a lion.

## Swanley Whattam (8)

Althorpe & Keadby Primary School, Keadby

# This Is Me

This is me...
I am as fast as a cheetah
I am a chameleon
My eyes are beautiful
I am as strong as a lion.

**Rhyley Whitlam (8)**
Althorpe & Keadby Primary School, Keadby

# This Is Me

This is me...
I am as strong as a wolf
I am a hippo
I am as funny as a hyena
I am chocolate orange.

## Brody G (8)
Althorpe & Keadby Primary School, Keadby

# About Sid

*A kennings poem*

A game player,
A Minecraft pro,
A snack lover,
A movie watcher,
A bike rider,
A noise maker.

**Sid Michael Alan Burgin (9)**
Althorpe & Keadby Primary School, Keadby

# Queen For A Day

If I were queen for a day,
It would start with a plateful,
Of perfect pancakes,
Smothered in plump strawberries,
Practically drowning in pleasurable passion fruit drinks.

If I were queen for a day,
The sparkling sun would never cease,
Seaside strolls would be superb,
Whilst listening to the sniggers of excited children,
Sculpting sandcastles with buckets and spades,
On seaweed free beaches.

If I were queen for a day,
I would move into a magnificent library,
With miles and miles of bookshelves,
Overflowing with magic, mayhem and mystery,
Maybe even miracles.

If I were queen for a day,
Teachers would tirelessly build me a towering, ten-storey treehouse,
So tall that it tickled the clouds above.

I think I'd like being queen for a day,
I'm not sure my teachers would though.

## Sophie Griffin (8)
Auriol Junior School, Stoneleigh

# Who Should I Be?

If I had to be anyone, who would I be?
My father, my mother, my sister or my brother,
Or a mixture of all, across my family tree,
Or maybe my dog Zucchini,
Running around and playing fetch,
Lying on his back and having a stretch.

If I had to be anyone, who would I be?
The prime minister of England,
Changing the world and making it more friendly,
Ruling England like a star,
In order to make the country and people go far,
Or a celebrity,
Out in the jungle, making some tea,
Or dancing the quickstep on Strictly.

If I had to be anyone, who would I be?
Unique and special,
Different from the rest,
Kind, caring and the best,
If I had to be anyone, who would I be?
I would choose to be me.

## Alessia Mouskoundi (7)
Auriol Junior School, Stoneleigh

# This Is Me

This is me, I am a superstar
I like to sing, dance and play
Arts and crafts are fun for me
Hula hooping I can do all-day

This is me, I am a fabulous foodie
Pizza I want, then pizza I get
Topped with peppers, olives and onions
My uncle Vin makes the best ones yet

This is me, I am a big daydreamer
A perfect piano teacher I wish to be
Or perhaps a dentist or an artist
I'm really great, can't you see?

This is me, I am a happy helper
My cheeky dimples make people smile
When I am blue my sister cheers me up
Happy or sad, my feelings change after a while.

This is me,
I am Elissa!

**Elissa Patel (8)**
Auriol Junior School, Stoneleigh

# Marvellous Millie

I start off with life and grow up as a child
I have lots of family and friends and they love me
like wild
This is the beginning, you wait and see
A poem all about me
I like building Lego like a bird builds its nest
I enjoy that because it is the best
I can run as fast as a cheetah chasing its prey
I can swim as far as a whale searching for his food
all day
I can dance like a flamingo, gracefully on one leg
I take care of my kittens and hold them like an egg
I can hang upside down on bars like a bat
I can handstand for hours, no other animal can do
that
I am marvellous Millie and all these things make
me.

## Millie Strudwick (9)

Auriol Junior School, Stoneleigh

# Gemma's Life

I am going to tell you a story,
Of a girl in Jamaica,
And her name is Gemma Maker,
She and her parents live on a farm,
Her mum was the baker,
And her dad made paper.

But school was a different story,
She got bullied by Adam Lory,
Calling her flea twit, freak kid, gory,
That was the least of her worries,
Because there are no food lorries,
So she wanted to make her mark,
By playing basketball in the park.

A few years later,
At the Olympic games,
Gemma got called up,
To play basketball,
How wrong was Adam Lory,
Because Gemma got the glory.

## Annie Rice
Auriol Junior School, Stoneleigh

# Me, Myself And I

I have one million teddy bears
Sometimes I trip right down the stairs
I like to eat chocolate eclairs
That's me, myself and I.

I draw, I paint, I will create
I hate it when I'm running late
I like to hang out with my mate
That's me, myself and I.

I'm really shy in crowded places
I'm nimble and I leave no traces
I'm very slow at tying laces
That's me, myself and I.

So this is me and don't forget
That all my traits I don't regret
And this is for the haters out there
Whatever you say I really don't care.

## Kali Napier (10)
Auriol Junior School, Stoneleigh

# THIS IS MEgan

My name is Megan Linch
My hair is long and brown
My eyes are shiny hazel
I never have a frown

My favourite sport is horse riding
I like dancing and gymnastics too
I like to collect Blue Peter badges
And a vet is what I want to do

My family is important
There are six of us in all
I am the oldest sibling
And my brothers just love dribbling

My cat is called Vlad
He loves to jump and play
His eyes are bright and green
And his fur is soft and grey.

**Megan Linch (8)**
Auriol Junior School, Stoneleigh

# Painting My Life

Art can show,
What we can't explain,
You can show happiness,
Or you can show pain.

Art can be anything,
Anything you dream of,
Or,
What you cannot dream of.

I am painting my life,
With colours so bright,
The mornings are blue, with yellow sunlight,
School is rainbow, red, pink, purple and green.

The things I learn,
On top of what I have seen,
This is why I am painting my life,
Like an artist, no, trying to be an artist.

**Melina Tuyluoglu (8)**
Auriol Junior School, Stoneleigh

# Things I Do And Don't Like

I like to play football down the park,
But I don't like to be alone in the dark,
I loved the beach in Broadstairs,
But I hated the long drive there,
It makes me happy to play the piano well,
But it makes me sad when I mess it up,
It makes me excited when I go around to my
friends',
But I am always tired when the playtime ends,
My sister can be annoying but I love her as much
as my mum and dad,
My family are what make me the happiest and
never sad.

**Dexter Newby-Walker (8)**
Auriol Junior School, Stoneleigh

# I Think I Am Amazing!

I think I am amazing, in fact, I am quite unique,
I like to laugh and joke with friends,
I have a bit of a quirky streak.

I think I am amazing, I could sing and dance all
day,
I am quite the fashionista,
In every single way.

I think I am amazing,
I try my best, it's true,
My favourite food is sushi and I like skateboarding
too.

I think I am amazing,
I hope you all agree,
This poem describes everything fabulous about
me!

**Connie Shepherd (9)**
Auriol Junior School, Stoneleigh

# Who I Am

My name is Rocco and I am seven,
My favourite holiday is down in Devon.

I like to eat rare steak,
On my lunch break.

In my spare time I play golf,
And my favourite reindeer is Rudolph.

When I grow up I want to be a vet,
With my own private jet.

I love my twin sister,
When I'm not with her I miss her.

My brother is my best friend,
I will love him until the end.

## Rocco Pillay (7)
Auriol Junior School, Stoneleigh

# This Is All About Me

My name is Sienna,
I am in Year Three,
I am in Amber Class,
And I love doing tasks,

I love dogs,
And walking on logs,
I love searching for insects,
And reading lots of texts,

I love picking up sand,
In my hands,
I try my hardest not to talk and walk,

This is me and I have to agree,
There is no one like me,
Because we are all unique,
In our own special way.

**Sienna Amin (7)**
Auriol Junior School, Stoneleigh

# Eva

**E** very day I love to sing
**V** ery happy as I dance along
**A** nd make up my new routine

**G** ymnastics is my favourite sport
**R** ound offs, cartwheels and backbends
**U** pon the monkey bars I love to hang
**T** esting my strength every day
**Z** ipping up and down
**N** ever giving up
**E** ven when my hands are sore
**R** eady for my next adventure.

## Eva Grutzner (7)
Auriol Junior School, Stoneleigh

# This Is Us

This is me, this is he and this is she
I like bananas, he likes farmers and she likes to go
on holiday to the Bahamas
This is I, this is him and this is her
I like my dog, he likes his warthog and she likes her
pet frog
This is us
You might think this, you might think that
He will sit, she has a cat
You might be a mad hatter
But all of that doesn't matter
Because we are all different.

## Samuel Webb (9)
Auriol Junior School, Stoneleigh

# This Is Me

Sometimes, I feel yellow, happy and bright, other times I feel blue, downhearted with no delight
Winter makes me glow when I'm playing in the snow
My cats bring me joy when they're being good boys, especially when they're playing with me and their toys
I love being with my friends, playing and laughing until the day ends, but most important to me is spending precious time with my family.

## Lilah Piper (8)
Auriol Junior School, Stoneleigh

# Who Am I?

**W** hen knowing me you'll know that I'm kind, sensitive and generous

**H** ow I do art is with my heart, and I put lots of effort into it

**O** n special occasions, I like to dress up and put lots of clips in my hair

**A** pples are my favourite fruit

**M** y family are important to me

**I** am very different and unique, well, that's a good thing.

## Evie Makinson (10)

Auriol Junior School, Stoneleigh

# Me

Don't tell me who I am meant to be
I am free and I know me
I will do as I am told
But if it is wrong I will be bold
I will try my best
And take on any test
I will be a good friend
Until the very end
I will hold my head high
And smile as you go by
So don't tell me who I am meant to be
I am free and I know me.

## Henry Saunt (9)
Auriol Junior School, Stoneleigh

# This Is Me

**T** all for my age
**H** air that is short and ginger
**I** like to play sports with my friends
**S** chool is my favourite place to be

**I** love English, maths and science
**S** inging and dancing are some of the best things

**M** aybe I'll be an author when I'm older
**E** mily is my name.

**Emily Benzeval (7)**
Auriol Junior School, Stoneleigh

# Me And My Life

I'm funny and kind but crazy in the mind,
I like the gym and love to swim,
I have a dad and a sister and a mum,
And a dog that's really fun,
She's called Roxy and is very energetic,
She couldn't possibly be more perfected,
This is me and I choose who to be,
This is me and I choose who to be.

## Daniella Foxcroft (10)
Auriol Junior School, Stoneleigh

# All About Ava

**T** houghtful and caring to animals
**H** elpful at all times
**I** love to read and read and read!
**S** tories make me cheerful inside

**I** want to have a dog one day
**S** nuggly, soft and super fun

**M** y friends are incredibly important to me
**E** very single one!

## Ava Dockery (7)
Auriol Junior School, Stoneleigh

# Me

I like video games
I play them all the time
I like going on roller coasters
Because they go so fast
I nearly got my head knocked off
Please make it stop
I love playing football
I love playing in a team
My mum comes to watch me
Which makes Saturday morning a dream.

**Josh Lines (8)**
Auriol Junior School, Stoneleigh

# This Is Me

I'm sometimes funny
Hungry and if I don't take my medicine
My nose is really runny

When I grow up
I want to be a gymnast
And make lots and lots of money

My favourite month is April
Because I get lots of chocolate
From the Easter bunny.

**Jessica Beattie (7)**
Auriol Junior School, Stoneleigh

# My Brother

My brother's name is LJ
I used to call him way way
He plays Minecraft all day long
He doesn't like it when I sing a song
He goes to high school, he's eleven
He is, in Year 7
LJ is the best big brother
I definitely do not want another.

**Harrison Plant (8)**
Auriol Junior School, Stoneleigh

# This Is Me

My name is Sienna, I like to dance
I also like to sing and prance
I have blue eyes and ginger hair
Some people say it is very rare
What I like the most
Is my daddy's Sunday dinner roast
I have a younger brother
And I love him like no other.

## Sienna Culm (7)
Auriol Junior School, Stoneleigh

# Double Digits

My name is Lola
I love drinking cola
Best with ice
It tastes so nice
I'm turning ten, time to leave the one-digit den
I still like my fidgets, even in double digits
That's enough about me, time to drink my bubble
tea.

## Lola Howes (10)
Auriol Junior School, Stoneleigh

# Live Your Life Like Nature

**N** ature is what makes me happy
**I** nsects buzzing around
**A** nimals leaping and pouncing
**L** ions snoozing and leopards cruising
**L** ife should be lived this way!

## Niall Smit (9)

Auriol Junior School, Stoneleigh

# Frank

**F** ootball is my favourite sport

**R** ocking the game

**A** lways try my best

**N** obody can stop me

**K** icking to beat the rest.

## Frank Linch (7)

Auriol Junior School, Stoneleigh

# My Favourite Animal

My favourite animal is nice and fluffy,
She runs around and is very funny,
She makes a noise that sounds weird,
When we go out she is not happy,
She plays with another animal but it doesn't like her,
We go outside and play with toys,
She sometimes acts like a boy,
When I go to bed she sits and stares,
She skids across the floor,
Sometimes she can't stop,
She hates cars,
When we go for a little stroll she knows where to go,
Who is it?

Answer: My dog Roxy.

**Marlie Bailey (8)**
Barcroft Primary School, Barcroft

# All About Me

**T** his is me, kind and generous
**H** ave some differences from others
**I** really love my family
**S** ometimes I like to play football

**I** like to watch TV and go on bike rides with my family
**S** ometimes on the banks I explore and climb trees

**M** e and my little brother like playing together
**E** very day I wake up to come to school, except on the weekends.

## Mansa Kaur Chahal (8)
Barcroft Primary School, Barcroft

# My Favourite Game

**P** erfect at catching them

**O** ddish is an easy Pokémon to get

**K** akuna evolves into Beedrill

**E** volutions make a new Pokémon

**M** agikarp is a really jumpy Pokémon

**O** nix is a rock and is hard to get

**N** idoking and Nidoqueen spawn in one spot

**S** hinies are hard to get.

## Colby-Blu Read (8)

Barcroft Primary School, Barcroft

# This Is Me

**A** hamster is my favourite animal
**M** usic is my favourite subject
**A** pizza s my favourite food
**N** ever have I ever been mean
**D** rums are my favourite instrument
**E** ncouraging people is what I like
**E** ven I like to make people laugh
**P** ets are the cutest and I'm a pet lover.

## Amandeep Kaur (8)
Barcroft Primary School, Barcroft

# Liverpool

The goalkeeper is Allison
The captain is Henderson
The star player is Salah
The person who scores goals is Sadio Mane

The substitute for Henderson is Origi
The second star player is Roberto Firmihno
The other captain is Virgil Van Dijk
The coach is Jurgen Klopp
What is this team?

Liverpool.

**Akaal Singh Dhillon (8)**
Barcroft Primary School, Barcroft

# What I Am Good At And I Like

I am good at football in my team,
I am a really big chocolate eater,
I am a really good bike rider on my bike,
My favourite food is tuna and sweetcorn,
I am really good at free kicks and penalties,
I like fishing with my brother,
I like playing with my dogs,
I like playing FIFA 22 with my friends.

**Ethan Gregory (8)**
Barcroft Primary School, Barcroft

# This Is How To Make Me

First, put all six full jars of Christmas powder
Next, put holy water in me
Then get a spoon and mix
After put a drop of light red paint
Thirty minutes later get a large spoon and mix
some more
Finally, put six drops of F1 powder in
And that's how you make me.

**Jovan Ashan (8)**
Barcroft Primary School, Barcroft

# This Is Me

I love chocolate and sometimes sneak it
I love playing on the trampoline and sometimes
jump on it
I love playing with my family
With my family we like to play
And when we play we say yay
I like to play in the day
I went to the farm and jumped in hay.

## Lotti Harrison (9)

Barcroft Primary School, Barcroft

# This Is Riley

I look cute
I wear clothes
I cook food
I feel happy
I wear pink
I don't want to be silly
I only do my chores
We do our best
I am a helper
I am a kind girl who always helps buddies
I am a worker
I bake food.

**Riley Morris (8)**
Barcroft Primary School, Barcroft

# A Riddle

What is it?
It is something loud and high volume that you can dance to
You can sing to and listen to
And you can make discos
You can use instruments
To make sounds and sound players can make sounds.

Answer: Music.

## Carla-Maria Berechet (8)
Barcroft Primary School, Barcroft

# Riddle Poem

It is a fast swimmer
It lives in the water
It has very sharp teeth
It has a light on its head
It is at the bottom of the sea
It has bright eyes
It is a carnivore.

Answer: Anglerfish.

**Bradley Thomas Dunn (8)**
Barcroft Primary School, Barcroft

# Ekam

I like to watch cartoons on the TV,
I love bacon, it is my favourite food,
I like food, it is good for you,
I love to watch TV,
I like to have something on the fridge,
I love Pepsi, it is my favourite soda.

## Ekam Singh Badyal (8)
Barcroft Primary School, Barcroft

# This Is Me

**S** porty at badminton
**O** nly like drawing flowers
**P** iano is my favourite thing to play
**H** ate bullies
**I** 'm a big book reader
**A** huge fool.

## Sophia Zaman (8)

Barcroft Primary School, Barcroft

# How To Make Me

This is how to make me
First, you sprinkle kindness, emotional support
Now add moves
Now add fun
Now add helping others and family
I'm never going to be cruel to anyone.

## Riley Makin (8)
Barcroft Primary School, Barcroft

# Riddle

It is black and white
And it might give you a fright
It is big and fluffy and it eats a lot of plants
Sometimes its tongue is long.

Answer: Anteater.

**Perran Peters (8)**
Barcroft Primary School, Barcroft

# Jasroop

Sometimes it can be angry
It is an animal
It is very big
Sometimes it could be in a zoo.
What is it?

Answer: A lion.

## Jasroop Singh (9)
Barcroft Primary School, Barcroft

# This Is Me

Whale in the water
Cat lover
Fast as a lion
Typical at gaming
Strong as a lion
Silent reader.

This is me!

## Logan Seaton (8)
Barcroft Primary School, Barcroft

# My Fun Fantastic Life

My name is Jack and I live down Pudding Lane
I have a guinea pig called Custard and he has a
little mane
Dirty Bertie, playing with his pals
Rolling in fox poo and messing all around
Plastic and pollution, it makes me very mad
Put your rubbish in the bin, stop making me sad
Over ramps
Under bridges, trying not to fall into ditches
I hope you think my words are wise
And send my school the very best prize!

**Jack Watson (9)**
Snainton CE Primary School, Snainton

# Me

My name is Hannah
I have a dog called Nell
She is silly but friendly as well
A rabbit called Fluffy
Who's funny and fat
A guinea pig called Muffin
My brother is called Christopher
He's funny and tall
Telling jokes and stating facts
Educating us all
I don't like swimming or football
It bores me almost to death
Please pick my poem about me
And my school will be impressed!

**Hannah Boynton (8)**
Snainton CE Primary School, Snainton

# Things About Me

My hair is as thin as a stick
My hair is as brown as fudge
As a child, I'm going through challenging stuff
My eyes are as hazel as a flower
My love of roller skating keeps me slow and steady
I'd like to be a robin that goes *tweet, tweet, tweet*
My bed makes me relaxed and calm
My love goes to my family and friends
If I could choose happiness I would surely do that.

**Katy Goodrick (8)**
Snainton CE Primary School, Snainton

# This Is Me

Bored is the worst feeling
Blasting on my bike is the best
Kasper and Ellie are my friends
Who put me to the test
Science is cool
My favourite thing in school
Sticky snails and scary spiders
Make me shake and shiver
Please pick my poem
I've tried so hard to use my brain and pen
If I win I'll be so happy
And do it all again.

## Connie Harber (7)
Snainton CE Primary School, Snainton

# Holidays

H appy holidays here and there,

O ver open mountain ranges,

L icking lollipops when I am tired,

I ce for warm days,

D roopy dogs running around the garden,

A fun wild walk over hills and mountains,

Y o-yos look different everywhere I go,

S uper slimy slime, sliding everywhere.

## Oskar Bond (8)
Snainton CE Primary School, Snainton

# This Is Me

**T** he very fluffy dogs make me happy,
**H** appiness is the best,
**I** love my family and friends,
**S** lithery snakes are scary,

**I** 'm very passionate about dogs and cats,
**S** mall things are my thing,

**M** arshmallows I like a lot,
**E** ating mushrooms are my favourite.

## Jessica Hodgson (10)
Snainton CE Primary School, Snainton

# This Is Me

My name is Clifford
People call me Cliff
I like spicy chips
Doritos are the best
Baby sloths are so cute
Kittens are too
Laughing, prancing, the joke's on you
Plastic pollutions make me mad as hell
Just pick up rubbish put it in the bin
Wash your tubs, clean your tins.

## Clifford Akrill (7)
Snainton CE Primary School, Snainton

# Animals

Cats and dogs are my number one,
Guinea pigs are also fun,
Mice and hamsters are great,
Me and my pets are special mates,
Horses and ponies are fun to groom,
Especially when I do it in my room,
I feel elated when I see my pets,
But I feel devastated when they go to the vets.

## Charleigh Jones (10)
Snainton CE Primary School, Snainton

# Family And Happiness

My hair is straight and as bright as the sun
My eyes are as blue as the skies
I'm strong, brave and tall
And love having lots of fun

I love pretty ponies
Teddies tumbling off my bed
Walking with my dogs
One, two, three
Nala, Star and Ruby with my family.

**Imogen Parkin (8)**
Snainton CE Primary School, Snainton

# Guinea Pigs

My name is Scarlett and I like red
Flamingos and guinea pigs are in my head
I have them on my walls, in my bed, on my clothes
They are in my head wherever I go
Friends are important
Zayn, Charleigh, Hollie and Caine
Going out on my bike
Even in the rain.

**Scarlett Freer (9)**
Snainton CE Primary School, Snainton

# I Like

My eyes are hazel
My hair is blonde
I like Lego and football
And looking into ponds

Getting COVID would be a pest
And stops my fun and play
Choose my poem, I've tried real hard
And really make my day.

**Kasper Reeve (7)**
Snainton CE Primary School, Snainton

# This Is Me

My name is Christopher
I have a sister
She is very silly and daft
She pokes the dog and makes me laugh
Mum tried to watch Strictly
While Hannah, cha-cha-cha'd
It wasn't the best
I wonder what's next?

**Christopher Boynton (9)**
Snainton CE Primary School, Snainton

# Horses

**H** appy is the best feeling in the world
**O** ceans swimming with the horses
**R** iding is my passion
**S** ophie is my sister
**E** xcited to take a prize
**S** hould I impress you with my skills?

## Madelaine Jenkins (8)
Snainton CE Primary School, Snainton

# About Me

My name is Jessica
Any type of animal is what I love
Not dangerous ones as they scare me too much
My eyes are like the ocean
My hair is brown and straight
Living with eight dogs means not much to play!

## Jessica Berry (10)
Snainton CE Primary School, Snainton

# Motorcross

My eyes are as blue as the sea
Motorcross is me
I'm as fast as lightning on the bike
As a cheetah in the night
I need to be a motocross star
Hoping and dreaming I'll go far!

**Oliver Osborne (10)**
Snainton CE Primary School, Snainton

# My Life

My eyes are as dark as a black hole
My interests are spirits and ghosts
Black cats are
My lucky charm
My favourite is my family
And my computer
I love the most.

**Isaiah Jones (7)**
Snainton CE Primary School, Snainton

# To Create My Silly Self

You will need...
Endless laughter
A sprinkle of joy
A truckful of snow
A bucketful of strawberries
A roomful of ice cream

Now you need to...
Firstly, grab your bucketful of strawberries and your roomful of ice cream and mix them gently
Secondly, add your truckful of snow and your endless laughter and stir thoroughly
After that, get what you have so far and cook in the oven at forty degrees for thirty minutes
Make sure it's crispy
Once cooked, sprinkle your joy on top
Voila, you're done!

## Mollie-Mae Brown (10)
Walgrave Primary School, Walgrave

# My Recipe

Ingredients:
A tablespoon of chatter
A pinch of ambition
A size four football
A handful of humour
A drizzle of friendship
A kilogram of coolness
A teaspoon of silliness
A pack of wine gums
A Manchester United shirt

Pour a tablespoon of chatter into a bowl with the size four football and the pack of wine gums
Then mix thoroughly until a watery texture
Next, in a separate bowl grab the handful of humour and drop it into the separate bowl
Then put it in the oven for four minutes and nine seconds
Now, go back to your old bowl
Cut up the kilogram of coolness into bite-size squares
Arrange them into a smiley face on top of the mixture

Add a teaspoon of silliness to the main bowl
Now take the separate bowl out of the oven
Sprinkle on a pinch of ambition and drizzle some
friendship around the sides
After you have done all that
Let the separate bowl mixture flow into the main
bowl
Leave it for roughly two minutes for both mixtures
to combine
Now carefully lay the Manchester United shirt over
everything and wait a day for it to set
Now you have me.

## Ewan McGillivary (11)
Walgrave Primary School, Walgrave

# My Fabulous Recipe

To make me you will need...
A cup of loyalty
A pair of football boots
Five heaped teaspoons of creativity
An everlasting stack of books
A creme caramel
A positive attitude
A saucer of smallness
A Harry Potter film
A raspberry cheesecake
A warm heart

Now you need to...
Tip five tablespoons of creativity into a large
mixing bowl,
Then stir a pair of football boots into the mixture,
Add your everlasting stack of books and pour a
saucer of smallness,
Mix thoroughly with an electric whisk,
In a different bowl, combine the Harry Potter
movie, the raspberry cheesecake and the creme
caramel,

Cook in the oven until golden and an inserted skewer comes out clean,
Whilst the cake is cooking, prepare an icing with a positive attitude, warm, heart and enormous smile by creaming it up with a whisk,
Once the cake is cooled, spread the icing over the cake with a spatula,
Now sprinkle the loyalty over the icing for a finishing touch.

## Martha Burchell (10)

Walgrave Primary School, Walgrave

# How To Create Me

You will need...
A sprinkle of naughtiness
A world of football and grass
Endless mischief
A bundle of silliness
A bar of delicious Daim
A page of a football annual
VIP tickets to Chelsea Women

Now you need to:
Get the bundle of silliness and the VIP tickets,
Next, you beat them together until white and creamy,
Second, you need a separate plastic bowl to melt the bar of Daim,
When you tip it in make sure to leave the bowl warm,
After, rip the page of the annual into tiny bits and let that stand,
While the tiny bits of annual are left to stand, tip the world of football and grass into the other ingredients in the plastic bowl,

It should be soft,
When all the ingredients are in the bowl, add the
endless mischief,
Next, tip the ingredients into a round-shaped tin
and cook at forty degrees, for about half an hour
until squidgy and crispy,
Then sprinkle over the naughtiness,
You're done!

## Imogen Perkins (11)
Walgrave Primary School, Walgrave

# How To Make Me

To make me you will need...
An enormous bar of Dairy Milk chocolate
A bundle of respect
A heap of kindness
Endless activities
10kg of sports
A truckload of love
5kg of books

Now you need to...
Preheat the oven to 170 degrees
Following that, mix the bundle of respect with the heap of kindness until light and creamy
In a separate bowl, sift in the truckload of love with the 5kg of books
Next, tip half of the endless activities into each bowl and stir with a fork
After that, pour both bowls into a large baking tray and slowly add the 10kg of sports
Finally, crush up the enormous bar of Dairy Milk chocolate and place it in the oven for twenty minutes

Make sure you take it out at the exact time or it will not work
There, you have made me!

## Lucie Cawston (9)
Walgrave Primary School, Walgrave

# This Is Me

I love food,
After it, I'm in a good mood,
I lounge in the sun,
I'm always down to have fun.

I'm super daring,
I'm speedy on the wing,
I love climbing trees,
I care for bees.

I am really loud,
When you see me play football you will be wowed,
I'm a go-kart king,
I love gaming.

I love cars,
I'm so strong, I can break iron bars,
You'll see me in a hot tub or playing cricket,
I'm so good I always hit the wicket.

I love Halloween,
I'm never mean,

I'm super chatty,
I'm as fast as a Bugatti.

There is no animal in the world I don't like,
I love my bike,
I love Mother Ivey,
And this is me.

**Thomas Sweeney (10)**
Walgrave Primary School, Walgrave

# My Recipe

To create me you will need:

A milk chocolate bar,
A truckload of happiness,
A bowl of giggles,
And finally, a bootful of respect.

Now you need to...

Crush the bar of milk chocolate and put it to one side.
Next, pour the bowl of giggles into the tray and gently tap it with your pinky until smooth like sand.
Then, lift the bootful of respect and carefully pour it in.
Do not spill it or it will not work,
Following on, tip the truckload of happiness into the tray and gently stir with your other pinkie until all the crumbs are broken into a flat texture.
Now, bake in the oven until crispy golden.

Finally, sprinkle on the crushed chocolate bar. Let it set until cool.

This is me!

## Ella Sargent (10)
Walgrave Primary School, Walgrave

# How To Make Me

You will need...
A bucket of respect
A truckful of kindness
A houseful of happiness
A box of silliness
A handful of gaming

Now you need to...
Get your biggest bowl out
Put your bucket of respect in the bowl
Blend it for five seconds,
Next put in the truckful of kindness and stir it for
thirty seconds,
Dump a houseful of happiness
Get one handful of gaming and silliness and
sprinkle it on
Now you have me.

## Mark Spatcher (9)
Walgrave Primary School, Walgrave

# This Is Me

**I** ndependent at doing my homework
**R** easonable at explaining
**E** nergetic at doing sports
**N** eat at tidying
**E** arly riser

**A** mazing at art
**L** oyal taking care of my sister
**V** olunteering to help people
**A** thletic at sports
**R** eliable to friends
**E** nthusiastic to people
**Z** esty being with friends!

This is me!

## Irene Alvarez (9)
Walgrave Primary School, Walgrave

# This Is Me

**J** olly like my dogs when they get food
**E** nergetic to my football team when I'm in goal
**N** eat like a dog in a dog show
**S** on of Jen
**O** ptimistic like an athlete
**N** ation friendly

**B** east at goalkeeping
**U** nbelievable at listening
**D** aft like a shark eating kelp
**D** ecent like a big, fluffy dog.

This is me!

## Jenson Budd (9)

Walgrave Primary School, Walgrave

# Why I'm Joyful

Joyful comes out a lot,
Normally when people are kind,
Angry it is not,
It can live outside or in your mind,

It likes to run about,
And turn your frown upside down,
It will sneak out,
To go and play around,

Joyful is a good emotion,
And may I add,
It takes time and devotion,
But you will never be sad,
That's why I'm joyful!

**Faith Wharton (10)**
Walgrave Primary School, Walgrave

# All About Me

*A kennings poem*

I am a,
Strong swimmer,
Dog walker,
Intelligent thinker,
Creative writer,
Friendly speaker,
Brave climber,
Active runner,
Strictly watcher,
Light sleeper,
Popcorn eater,
Good helper,
Halloween lover,
Book reader,
This is me!

## Mackenzie Thomas Wainwright (10)

Walgrave Primary School, Walgrave

# The Things About Me

**E** xcellent every day
**L** ively like a tiger
**L** oud like a lion
**Y** oung like a turtle

**M** ischievous at home
**A** thletic like a swimmer
**E** nergetic like a dog

This is me.

## Elly-Mae Potts (10)
Walgrave Primary School, Walgrave

# A Poem That Describes Me

*A kennings poem*

I am a
Bouncy mover
Happy thinker
Contagious smiler
Light sleeper
Early riser
Chocolate eater
Hard worker
Horse rider
Sporty runner
Team player
And finally an amazing friend.

## Isla Mulligan (10)

Walgrave Primary School, Walgrave

# This Is Me

**D** angerous and daring,
**E** nergetic like a puppy,
**V** ehicle lover,
**L** oud speaker,
**Y** awning like a tiger,
**N** umber minded.

## Devlyn Morrison (10)
Walgrave Primary School, Walgrave

# As Wild As Me

As wild as me,
I call maths, it's the key,
Football is my best friend,
Always until the end,
I am fantastic at algebra,
It's because I'm smart, duh.

As wild as me,
I can count, one, two, three,
Always with my little sis,
She always takes the mick,
When I'm in school six hours a day,
Don't want to go home because it's too cray.

As wild as me,
Too scared to go in the sea,
Always on the sand,
I stand on the land,
Maybe if I went there,
I wouldn't be that scared.

As wild as me,
I really like cheese,
I have really blonde hair,
And I don't think they care,
With my pearly blue eyes,
I can really count mice,
With my clear green glasses,
I don't care what they think,
As wild as me!

## Laci Phillips (10)

Ysgol Calon Y Dderwen, Newtown

# This Is Me! Bradley

This is me, a ten-year-old baker,
And 100 per cent no haters,

I may look like a small midget,
But I'm good at maths, digit by digit,

My hair is brown as poo,
Yes, the kind you find in the loo,

My eyes are the great blue ocean,
But definitely not the emotion,

My dad can be rotten,
But can be nice as pollen,

My mum is a favourable flower,
And lovely as an admirable panda,

I'm a sneaky fox,
But not as strong as an ox,

My glasses are a glorious navy,
And I don't mind a bit of gravy,

I'm a creative theme park creator,
But I'm not a very crafty maker,

So now you know everything about me
And now I will give you permission to go for a wee.

## Bradley Mitchell (10)
Ysgol Calon Y Dderwen, Newtown

# I'm Leo

I am a Liverpool fan,
I love to watch them play,
In the league and Champions League every
Saturday.

I am a better penalty taker than Mo Salah,
A superior goalkeeper to Allison,
And a worthier captain than Henderson.

I am an amazing swimmer,
I swim as fast as a fish,
I have more medals than Tottenham players.

My eyes are as blue as the ocean,
My hair is as blonde as a buttercup,
I am as short as a goblin.

I am as funny as Rob Beckett,
I'm a really good FIFA player,
I always beat my dad.

Family is as precious as a diamond,
I have two evil baby sisters,
They are a bit of a handful but I love them.

**Leo Andrews (11)**
Ysgol Calon Y Dderwen, Newtown

# My Recipe

I need...
Five spoons of friends
Eleven pounds of happiness
A spot of sad times
A pinch of silliness
A sprinkle of arguments
Three quarters of a cup filled with things that
make me happy
And finally a drop of brown food colouring for my
bold brown mane-like hair

I will only take a bit of time to cook and trust
But that is okay
Whilst baking, you will see me rising with
enjoyment and intensity
Decorating with icing and sprinkles makes me look
perfect
When you cut me open I am filled with the best
friends, fun times and family filled memories
In the end, you will eventually turn out with me
This is me.

## Siena Salvati (11)
Ysgol Calon Y Dderwen, Newtown

# Just Me

My life is a wild jungle
Adventurous, psycho and unexpected
My hair is as yellow as
An autumn tree leaves
My eyes like the ocean
Big, blue and deep
Seeing many things
Things that you don't know
And when night comes, these eyes close
My mind dreaming on
I see dragons big and blue
And dwarves short not tall
The dreams I possess are hot and cold
Sweet and sour
Hideous and gorgeous
You might think I'm weird
For writing all these things
But you haven't seen this wild world, through my
ocean eyes

This is me
Just me
Not you
Me.

## Leal Borysiewicz (10)
Ysgol Calon Y Dderwen, Newtown

# This Is Me

I am a Liverpool legend,
I hear the joyful roaring crowd in the stadium,
I see the football fly high above me,
Into the top corner of the goal net,
My hair is a woolly mammoth,
With my murky brown eyes,
I wish I wasn't as ear-splitting as a howler monkey,
My favourite animal is a speedy cheetah,
I am scared of nothing,
I am a nature lover,
I like to watch butterflies flutter by,
I love the foster home that I live in now,
With my two dogs Peggy Mitchell and Teddy,
My name is Jayden Ridgeway and this is me.

## Jayden Ridgeway (10)
Ysgol Calon Y Dderwen, Newtown

# All About Me

My hair is brown and messy like a mop,
My eyes are like miniature muddy puddles,
I have glasses perched upon my nose,
I am funny, I make my friends laugh,
This is me,
Playing rugby, I am like a bullet across the field,
Tackling someone, I am like an angry lion chasing
its prey,
I dream of playing for Wales rugby team,
This is me,
I'm a farmer boy at heart,
I am always out and about,
Busy on the grassland,
There is always something to do,
I am happiest with my puppy called Chubs,
This is me.

## Aidan Owen (10)
Ysgol Calon Y Dderwen, Newtown

# I'm Alex

I am a
Great reader
Chocolate eater
Football player
I love it when bright red leaves fall from the trees
When I walk around a forest in the middle of
autumn
Dark brown hair like the coat of a bison
A very big jumper so I'm always warm
Deep grey eyes like a thunderstorm
I grow a large variety of plants
Shamrock, tulip, asparagus, fern, personally my
favourite is aloe vera
I like ancient Greece, Rome and even Norse
mythology
Now, these are the things that make up me.

## Alex Riordan (10)
Ysgol Calon Y Dderwen, Newtown

# This Is Me

A pinch of fire
A dash of autumn
Enveloped in a blanket of warmth
My hair cascaded like melted chocolate flowing
down an appetising dessert
This is me

A sprinkle of freckles like cinnamon
Crystal blue eyes are the icing on the cake
A room overflowing with books
This is me

Fireworks exploding in my mind
I'm a brave bear
You start to break the cake

When you take me out
See what you can make
This is me.

**Jamie-Lee Ainsworth (11)**
Ysgol Calon Y Dderwen, Newtown

# All About Me

I have blonde wavy hair
Like the glistening ocean
Eyes the colour of chocolate bars
Looking at the shiny stars
I dream that I could be a lovely bunny
Bunnies are as cute as my little old boots
A brother who helps make gorgeous games on
Roblox
I wonder if we could play Minecraft in real life
I imagine mining gemstones
Is this me?
Yes, it's me
This is me
I wonder who you could be...

**Kacey Jayne Dorrell (10)**
Ysgol Calon Y Dderwen, Newtown

# Muddy

A wild Maddie, preferably Muddy
It appears moody
Crooked and small
Wouldn't ever be scared of it at all
Until it needs to feed

It'll growl until growling hurts
But if you throw it a bone
Preferably not your own
Maybe make it feel at home
Give it a clean, run it a bath
And when it's hungry
Never cross its path

It's Muddy, it's Maddie, it is me.

## Maddie Meller (10)
Ysgol Calon Y Dderwen, Newtown

# This Is Me

I am as busy as a gardener
I am as tall as a teacher
I have big feet like a giant
I dream of being a police officer
I am as skinny as a stick
I am me

I am Mo Salah scoring a goal
I am Grandad hitting a hole in one
I am Kobe Bryant leaping twenty-five ft in the air
I am Dan Brigger scoring a try
I am Matt Jones doing a backflip on a bike
I am me.

## Charlie Cleaver (10)
Ysgol Calon Y Dderwen, Newtown

# This Is Me

I am a golfer
Blue eyes like the ocean
Hair the colour of leaves in autumn
A four foot eleven giant
Strong and kind
A ten-year-old boy
This is me

My hands grip onto a golf club
Hitting the ball 400 yards
Hoping to get a hole in one today
Hitting the ball onto the green
I am a golfer
This is me.

## Alfie Cleaver (10)

Ysgol Calon Y Dderwen, Newtown

# I Dream

I dream in my treehouse
Friends curled up in silky blankets
PJs are huddled in trees
Trees with chocolate orange leaves
Behind me is a gingerbread school
Gummy bears running away
Above me is a light moor
And illuminated stars
Friends sleeping
Time to wake up
This is me.

## Emily Jerman (10)
Ysgol Calon Y Dderwen, Newtown

# My Life

J oyful as a rainbow
A mbitious as The Rock, Dwayne Johnson
C ool as James bond

D rip king
A rtistic like Bob Ross
V icious like a wolf
I have a dog called Ted
E lvis is my favourite singer
S teak is my favourite food

L emurs are fast like me
E lephants are strong like me
W hales are good swimmers like me
I have a bearded dragon called Rex
S nakes are one of my favourite animals.

## Jac Davies Lewis (10)
Ysgol Gwaun Cae Gurwen, Gwaun Cae Gurwen

# This Is Me

**E** vie is the best
**V** room, vroom, I have hoovering
**I** love to do dance, rugby and gymnastics
**E** ats as slow as a slug

**W** alking my dog is the best feeling ever
**I** like to stay up late on the weekend
**L** illy is my cousin
**L** oves to go on a walk
**I** love my best friends and my family
**A** film night is my favourite
**M** y siblings are annoying
**S** leep-ins are the best.

## Evie Williams
Ysgol Gwaun Cae Gurwen, Gwaun Cae Gurwen

# My Life

J ack is my best friend

O asis is my favourite drink

R ight as Albert Einstein

D rip king

A rt is the best

N ana makes the best cookies

C hicken wings are the best

H alloween is the best

A mbitious as a jaguar hunting its prey

L emurs are as fast as me

L ions are fearless like me

I enjoy drums

S nakes are stealthy like me.

## Jordan Challis (10)
Ysgol Gwaun Cae Gurwen, Gwaun Cae Gurwen

# About Me

**S** teff hides in slides
**T** urkey is nice
**E** lvis is a good singer
**F** encing is a good sport
**F** ast & Furious is a good franchise
**A** frica is amazing
**N** arnia is cold

**D** istance learning was hard
**A** pples are the best fruit
**N** uts are hard for me to eat
**I** like McDonald's
**E** at broccoli
**L** eopards are faster than me.

## Steffan Thomas (10)

Ysgol Gwaun Cae Gurwen, Gwaun Cae Gurwen

# What Makes Me, Me

**L** eopards are my favourite

**O** asis is my favourite drink

**T** ikTok is my favourite

**I** 'm as clever as a dog

**O** range Fanta is nice

**S** howers are the best

**U** nique

**L** emons are my least favourite fruit

**L** ions are cool

**I** play chess

**V** ictorious is good

**A** rt is my hobby

**N** etflix is my favourite channel.

## Loti O'Sullivan (10)
Ysgol Gwaun Cae Gurwen, Gwaun Cae Gurwen

# This Is Me

**C** oca-Cola is the best drink
**H** andful of kindness
**R** iding my scooter makes me happy
**I** like pizza
**S** prinkle of emotions

**P** air of Adidas Predators
**R** ub in some funniness
**E** lephants are my favourite animals
**S** wansea is my favourite football team
**T** urkey is nice
**O** range is my favourite colour
**N** ice and happy.

## Chris Preston (10)

Ysgol Gwaun Cae Gurwen, Gwaun Cae Gurwen

# Ingredients

**J** am is sweet

**A** pples are nice

**M** y mum is the coolest mum ever

**E** at carrots, they're good for me

**S** teffan is my best friend

**G** ru is the best movie character ever

**R** abbits are my favourite animal

**A** n orange is sweet like jam

**V** inegar on chips

**I** like cheeseburgers

**L** oti is my best friend.

## James Gravil (10)
Ysgol Gwaun Cae Gurwen, Gwaun Cae Gurwen

# This Is Me

**A** lys is my pretty name
**L** amb is my favourite food, it is as tasty as ice cream
**Y** ear 4 is the best class yet
**S** eren is my friend

**E** ira is my beautiful middle name
**I** love watching TikTok under my pretty bed
**R** yan is in my class, he is so funny
**A** game of football is the best.

## Alys Eira Lewis-Jones (8)
Ysgol Gwaun Cae Gurwen, Gwaun Cae Gurwen

# This Is Me

**W** il is my name
**I** like my family and friends
**L** ucas is my cool friend

**D** an, my stepdad, is the best
**A** lys is my other friend
**V** enomous snakes are my favourite
**I** am the king of hide-and-seek
**E** lephants are my least favourite animals
**S** ometimes I run like a fox.

## Wil Davies-Lewis (8)
Ysgol Gwaun Cae Gurwen, Gwaun Cae Gurwen

# This Is Me

**C** orey is my name
**O** ranges taste nice
**R** unning is my favourite
**E** veryone is my friend
**Y** esterday was rainy

**E** ats as fast as a fox
**V** ans are as slow as a slug
**A** cat is as fast as a cheetah
**N** ight is as dark as a cave
**S** leeping good in the night.

## Corey Evans (9)

Ysgol Gwaun Cae Gurwen, Gwaun Cae Gurwen

# The Spookiest Night

**H** alloween is the best season ever,
**A** dash of spookiness,
**L** oud as a wolf,
**L** ook spooky on Halloween,
**O** ld ruins of houses and schools,
**W** orld is spooky on Halloween,
**E** veryone is so excited for Halloween,
**E** xciting the spooky season,
**N** othing beats Halloween.

**Gethin Ieuan Hollis James (10)**
Ysgol Gwaun Cae Gurwen, Gwaun Cae Gurwen

# This Is Me

**M** y name is Maddi and yes, it may be short

**A** nd I have fluffy hair and I hope you don't mind that it's bright

**D** iana or is it Briana Shay? It is a beautiful surname!

**D** ogs are my favourite and I love puppies

**I** 've turned nine in October and the month went so fast!

## Maddison Roberts (9)

Ysgol Gwaun Cae Gurwen, Gwaun Cae Gurwen

# I Am Ellie

Some people call me Ellie Jelly
It is a funny name, everyone thinks the same
My favourite colour is yellow
And I like jello
I like games and trains
Every time I run fast I have a blast
School is fun
In the sun.
I wear glasses in all my classes!

## Ellie Walker (9)
Ysgol Gwaun Cae Gurwen, Gwaun Cae Gurwen

# My Ingredients

A dash of shortness
A sprinkle of caring
A tablespoon of ginger
A splash of thoughtfulness
A pinch of fun
A teaspoon of braveness
A bottle of smart
A handful of kind and friendly
A plate of helpfulness
A bowl of supportiveness.

## Harley Davies (10)
Ysgol Gwaun Cae Gurwen, Gwaun Cae Gurwen

# The Perfect Mini Me

A sprinkle of happiness
Mixed with some kindness
A dash of smartness
A sprinkle of wildness
A bucketful of creativity
Sixty litres of adventure
Mix together to make a perfect mini me.

**Alex White (10)**
Ysgol Gwaun Cae Gurwen, Gwaun Cae Gurwen

# This Is Me

**D** illan is my name
**I** like playing football
**L** yla and Lily love running as fast as a fox
**A** fter school I take my dogs for a walk
**N** ike has the best sports shoes.

## Dilan Morgan
Ysgol Gwaun Cae Gurwen, Gwaun Cae Gurwen

# This Is Me

**P** lenty of fun when I am in the park with my friends

**O** ne day I would like to be a YouTuber

**P** oppy is the best

**P** arks are the best to play

**Y** ouTube is the best.

## Poppy Flood
Ysgol Gwaun Cae Gurwen, Gwaun Cae Gurwen

# This Is Me

**L** ucas is my cool name
**U** no is my favourite game
**C** ai and Will are my best friends
**A** m good at football and rugby
**S** nakes are my favourite animal.

## Lucas Johns (9)
Ysgol Gwaun Cae Gurwen, Gwaun Cae Gurwen

# This Is Me

**R** uby is my name
**U** sually I play with my friends at school
**B** ecause I am playful I have lots of friends
**Y** ellow is the colour of my socks.

## Ruby Osborne
Ysgol Gwaun Cae Gurwen, Gwaun Cae Gurwen

# YOUNG WRITERS INFORMATION

We hope you have enjoyed reading this book – and that you will continue to in the coming years.

If you're the parent or family member of an enthusiastic poet or story writer, do visit our website **www.youngwriters.co.uk/subscribe** and sign up to receive news, competitions, writing challenges and tips, activities and much, much more! There's lots to keep budding writers motivated!

If you would like to order further copies of this book, or any of our other titles, then please give us a call or order via your online account.

Young Writers
Remus House
Coltsfoot Drive
Peterborough
PE2 9BF
(01733) 890066
**info@youngwriters.co.uk**

Join in the conversation!
Tips, news, giveaways and much more!

 **YoungWritersUK** 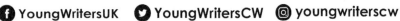 **YoungWritersCW** 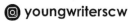 **youngwriterscw**